The Required Assembly

THE REQUIRED ASSEMBLY

Prose Poems by

Shivani Mehta

Press 53

Winston-Salem

Press 53, LLC
PO Box 30314
Winston-Salem, NC 27130

First Edition

A Tom Lombardo Poetry Selection

Copyright © 2025 by Shivani Mehta

Cover art, "Cracked," Copyright © 2012 by Ilbusca
Licensed through iStock

Cover design by Christine Garcia

Library of Congress Control Number
2024952297

ISBN 978-1-950413-92-8

For Sammy and Maya

Contents

Origin story 1   1

Ascension   2

The Invisible Girl wasn't always invisible   3

Invention of dreams   4

The only version we agree on   5

Places of worship   6

One year I lived alone   7

How to ride a dead horse   8

Subversion   9

The statues   10

Origin story 2   11

The mannequin   12

There was a time this could have been true   13

The Invisible Girl and the curiosity of strangers   14

Requiem   15

How to find your way out of the woods   16

Desire   17

Exodus   18

Between the wars   19

Revelation   20

Origin story 3   21

Homicide victims rarely talk to police   22

Sometimes I want to tell you   23

The Crow   24

The Bicycle   25

A form of directions   26

The Invisible Girl can be anything she wants when
    she doesn't want to be invisible   27

If I were an Agatha Christie villain   28

After the world has ended   29

A sonnet for the men I didn't love   30

Origin story 4   31

This is how I learned about regret   32

The required assembly   33

Notes on grief   34

How to eat an ice floe   35

Another one about the birds   36

Bible passages   37

The Invisible Girl goes to confession   38

The art of leaving   39

How to know when I'll be back   40

The babies   41

Postcard to an old lover   42

The encumbrance   43

Origin story 5   44

Genus and Species   45

The women who grew on trees   46

What the dead know   47

The Invisible Girl is a knifepoint against your throat   48

The Pawn Shop   49

After a line in a poem by Laura Kasischke   50

The craving   51

I'm beginning to think of the body as a well   52

Where Snow White is laid to rest   53

The education   54

The most important question   55

The sainthood   56

The catechism   57

The Invisible Girl knows   58

Origin story 6   59

Acknowledgments   61

Notes   63

Author Biograpghy   65

Origin story 1

My mother told me I was born from the sky, dropped from somewhere beyond the moon's shadow. She found me coiled on a crop of weeds, brushed the dirt from my body, shook worms from my hair.

Ascension

One summer, you walked your sadness on a leash the way
people walk a dog. Remember how, immune to gravity, it
floated somewhere above your right ear. At night the light was
bronze, reverent like the halos around dead saints. Children
tied balloons to your sadness, but it did not grow lighter.
And what I know of wildflowers, of regret, I learned while
standing beside your grave. We are made of glass. We carry
our dead behind closed eyes.

The Invisible Girl wasn't always invisible

When she was born the Invisible Girl was merely translucent, as if she were the daughter of a ghost or thin fog. Her favorite places in the house—doorways, open windows. The Invisible Girl feels a kinship with the wind. Sometimes she pretends that the wind is a girl named Effie. *Now Effie*, the Invisible Girl likes to say, *I'll hold this end of the curtain, you twirl it around like a scarf.*

Invention of dreams

A woman believes her shoes are wings. Every time she bends to tie her shoelaces, the woman closes her eyes and imagines she's an angel. She read in some bible or other that in order to achieve weightlessness, you have to empty yourself of every story, conviction, and crumpled napkin. She tries this while her husband sleeps, turns herself inside out like a pocket. This is how the dream was first invented—a woman suspended six inches above a bed, a man asleep in her shadow.

The only version we agree on

When we were together it never stopped raining. It would
have been different standing under an umbrella. What you
liked best was the curve of my spine under your hand.
Yesterday I sat on a park bench, three ants crawled up my
leg. There were no witnesses. After they crawled back down, I
climbed a tree, tied my scarf to a branch to see which way the
wind was blowing. In some languages the word for *compass*
rhymes with *alligator*. So much is unnamed, like the sound of
snow falling, or the way silence quivers like beads of water on
an unsteady surface. This is why I left. Afterwards, you said,
*it's hard to tell the difference between bone and rock with
your eyes closed.*

Places of worship

The aquarium, I go to often. Such a sense of belonging, of someone else's ecstasy, the kind you can buy in a back alley. Along with popcorn, they sell candles at the refreshment stand. I sit for hours without moving in front of the octopus tank, trying to think of words that rhyme with "come." *Thumb, strum*, the sound of the words is a prayer. Time can be everywhere at once. *Plumb*. I draw the word out as long as possible, like pressing the air from a paper bag. People stop to ask if I'm looking for something. I say, *look both ways when you cross the street*. Once, I said to the janitor as he swept around my feet, *look at that, slow-motion calligraphy of tentacles*. It reminded me of a black and white photograph I saw at a museum. A leafless tree in the snow, bare branches reaching wide as though trying to unhide itself.

One year I lived alone

I only had the moths for company, shared the flat with them.
How they clung to every surface like brown velvet petals.
How the night grew dark with their fluttering. Light filtered in
as if through a thick curtain. I grew accustomed to the gloom.
On cold nights we huddled in front of the fireplace, I under
a coarse blanket, moths forming a dark border around it like
sentinels. Sometimes I read aloud—to myself or them, I'm
still not sure—the sound of my voice soothed their trembling.
When I undressed for bed, their wings cast shadows on my
skin. They swirled around the room as I slept, alighting on my
thigh, an upturned palm, my closed eyes, like a kiss.

How to ride a dead horse

You can only attempt this while standing at the edge of a cliff with one way down, preferably under a full moon. A saddle is not essential, you can ride bareback. Falling at high speed is the same as falling in slow motion, both get you to the same place. This will be the closest you ever come to forgetting. To resurrect the dead, you must calculate the rate at which blood flows out of a gunshot wound on a battlefield. How long it takes a man to bleed to death. You must get to the body while it still holds some memory of being alive, like fragments of a broken window retain a memory of wholeness. You must reach the body before the soil beneath is loosened, before the grave is dug. If you hear the sound of hooves pounding the earth, the ground shaking with tremors, it's already too late.

Subversion

If only I'd been encouraged, as a child, to cultivate the ability
to breathe like a wren, that shallow, barely discernible rise
of its breast. Someone says *transmutation*. Or maybe *meet
me at the station*. Imagine each new footfall on the wooden
platform, the wait for a lover who never shows, hoarse cries
of steam engines. The moon is just another handsome face in
the dark. How the stars endure its relentless betrayal. How
the light loses itself in the sea's wilderness. If only I could
write letters to my other selves, the ones living their lives
alongside mine. The ones whose presence, on cloudy days, I
sense in the hastening of air against my cheek.

The statues

We eat grass when no one is looking. Sometimes a few
berries. We've learned to wait, to chew without moving our
mouths. At the train station doors open and close, the sound
of footsteps like pebbles falling in a river. At night we let out
our ancient breaths, gather in the vacant streets. In front of
shop windows, we pause to look inside. Over there, lit by a
streetlamp, a pair of brown boots. There, a silver tea service
polished to high shine, a leather suitcase with metal clasp
glinting. We walk home before sunrise; our bodies leave trails
of fine white dust.

Origin story 2

My mother told me I came from the sea, washed up on shore
with fragments of coral, my body swaddled in seaweed. She
heard my cry in the tide's restless lisp.

The mannequin

I bought her at a garage sale because she looks just like me. I place her in various parts of the house depending on the time of day. Sometimes she's at the kitchen table in her bathrobe, a plate of eggs and newspaper in front of her. Other times she's kneeling on the lawn next to the flower bed, gardening hat on her head. Most evenings she sits on my bed with the eiderdown tucked around her, a vase of red poppies on the nightstand. Every night I brush her black hair, so dark it swallows light like the bottom of the sea. Sometimes she reads, a book open on her lap, head bowed. Her arms are always bent at the elbow, hands in front of her face like a surgeon waiting for her gloves. Every now and then I catch a glimpse of our reflections in the mirror, I'm never sure which of us is real. Mornings, when the light slices her body in half, turns her face lustrous, I think of alabaster *Madonnas* weeping in rapture.

There was a time this could have been true

The Woman Who Is Sawed in Half every night longs for a different name. *Panfila*, like her grandmother who had three breasts and became a fortune-teller. *Carlotta* after her mother, whose feet looked like hands. For hours each day, the Woman Who Is Sawed in Half gazes in the mirror, fingers tracing the black jagged seam spanning her waist like a belt. Sometimes after a show, unzipping her torso from her legs, the Woman Who Is Sawed in Half wonders if she is really two women. She remembers how she was pulled from her mother in two pieces, the doctors' bewilderment, her father's disappointment. More than anything, The Woman Who Is Sawed in Half dreams of a day when she will wake to find herself seamless. Then, she can trade in the circus life, its fishnet stockings and sequins. Then, she will be just like other women. The Woman Who Is Sawed in Half knows this is just a pipe dream, always beyond her reach. Her grandmother's words have lived for years under her skin, *without a name, loneliness cannot find you.*

The Invisible Girl and the curiosity of strangers

The Invisible Girl arrives home from school. Her bedroom
has turned into a museum, her mother sells tickets at the door.
Inside, a crowd of people gather at the foot of the Invisible
Girl's bed. They tug at the sheets, stroke the lace frills on her
pillow. The alarm clock on the Invisible Girl's nightstand is
passed around, the knob on its back turned. Across the room
people rifle through the Invisible Girl's chest of drawers.
A woman in a fur coat scans the titles of books on a shelf:
The Self According to Rene Descartes; *The Man Who Tried
to Weigh His Soul; Horticulture: A Beginner's Guide* (7th
Edition). In the Invisible Girl's bathroom, a man lifts the lid
on the toilet to peer inside. A woman caresses a bar of soap in
the shower. *Intriguing*, she says, raising her camera. Suddenly,
the Invisible Girl feels a tingling sensation—this is the closest
she'll ever come to being visible. The Invisible Girl wonders
if her insides look like the pages of her journals, pinned open
above her desk like butterflies in a display case.

Requiem

The ghost children are asleep on the landing again, the
outlines of their overlapped bodies blurry like a watercolor.
They come and go as they please. I knew they returned when
the lights flickered once, twice, during dinner. We stopped
eating, forks suspended halfway to our mouths. Silence is a
room in our house. More than anything, the ghost children
want to be real. They play hide and seek like living children.
Sometimes in the evenings, they rest their heads on my
shoulder, deflating balloons coming back to earth. At night
lying in bed, we hear words like *canticle, saints, resurrection*
sung in childish voices. The ghost children know they don't
belong here, they are the children we don't have. *Forgive our
trespass* they whisper and are gone.

How to find your way out of the woods

Find an oak tree with a hidden door. Knock twice. If it opens, head north. If it stays closed and the ground under your feet begins to crumble, head south. Don't fall asleep in the tall grass, reeds swaying like girls' thin bodies. Feel the tug of hunger like a hand pulling you forward. Your dreams will be full of scorpions. Find the monk whose body is tattooed with the words of psalms. *Put away your lament, darkness never forgets you.* The voice inside you was never your own. Selah.

Desire

Tell me what you hold dear, and I'll tell you what came before, what comes after. The weather for instance, a flock of seagulls flying south in a perfect vee. And tell me how you lit a match, set fire to the clouds. I'll show you how I hold the night under my blouse, I'll let you glide your hands under my skin. And one day the dog will not be the dog, but the salty ash on someone's tongue. One day we'll wake with the taste of tulips in our mouths, daylight scorching our throats.

Exodus

When we were exiles, my mother wrapped me in paper bags
for warmth, carried me on her back as she walked for miles.
Our shadows on the ground were one body, everything I saw
was framed by her long black hair. Sometimes we stopped in
villages for shelter, never stayed for more than a night. We
weren't searching for anything holy, just a place where we
could uncurl our fists. My mother told me I was born with
the map on my back. I remember how, when we were lost,
she used it to orient herself, her coarsened fingers undoing the
buttons of my dress, smoothing the cloth from my shoulders,
cities and towns asleep under her fingers. Once she said, *Your
spine is the river, each vertebra is a path we could take.*

Between the wars

We keep the wounded and sick underground, in rooms without windows. Children are born who know nothing of sunlight, like sand in the desert knows nothing of rain. Their pale skin illumines the darkness, a vat of milk in the shadow of a barn. We sleep in shifts, build fires for warmth out of anything flammable. We wish people's mouths would become doors. Memory is a curse. Once, a stray cat climbed down an air shaft, meowed for three days. In this place, a murder of crows is a message. A few have left, followed train tracks out of the city. We watch until their bodies become specks, try not to blink until our vision starts to blur.

Revelation

We wrap our dead in familiar clothes, a shroud of old rags,
reeds, twigs, carry them up to the surface. Like wolves, we fill
the sky with our howls. It is hard to come back to the thin,
inhospitable air.

At night we gather, share stories about the way things were.
There is no sense of day or night. When we sleep it is so quiet we
can hear the symphony of hearts beating together. Each waking
is the same as every other. Some still pray, though no god has
ever found us here. Children play games, like how many times
they can circle a fire without getting scorched by flames.

Origin story 3

My mother told me I was born from the seed of a pistachio nut. She planted it in the garden and waited. Once a day she squeezed my body, testing for ripeness. When I grew to the size of an avocado she plucked me from the branches, peeled the leaves from my skin like an orange.

Homicide victims rarely talk to police

I'm good at translating, finding things that are lost. Don't
need a flashlight to find my way out of a sinking car. I'm a
train passing through the station, days go by without me. My
favorite color is black, which is to say, anything can happen.
When I stop being a train, I could be a detective. Who d'ya
think keeps a bullet from finding you? Sometimes the best
ending is a boat dredging the riverbed. I'll tell you this one
thing: your life is a curtain. I don't know who shot me but I'm
the dead man under the floorboards. You'll know me by the
loose change in my pocket.

Sometimes I want to tell you

My favorite place to make love is near a chimney. In some parts of the world, brides wear veils sewn from smoke. It's not because they're poor. In some parts of the world, eating the flesh of an avocado signifies loss of virginity. What you don't know is, sometimes with your lips pressed to the corner of my mouth, your hands molding my hips, I'm thinking of constellations buried in the ground without names. If I could press you between the pages of a book like some dead flower, I would. Remember when I tried to say "gone," but what came out was "go"? Remember how I coaxed the flavor of rum from your tongue?

The Crow

My lover brings me a loaf of bread instead of flowers. I place
it on the nightstand, glance at it while we're in bed. How
effortlessly bread holds its shape, how certain of its boundaries.
He might have sliced it, I think, as his lips trace my breast.
Outside the window there's a crow in a tree. I watch his
silhouette as he watches our shadows converging on the wall.
My eyes, closed for an instant, the graze of teeth. When I open
them the crow's gone. The spread of wings, the rapid rise into
darkness. Everything becomes something else. A scarecrow
sways in a wheat field, straw arms raised, begins to dance.

The Bicycle

One morning I wake to find I've turned into a bicycle. At work, people notice. They talk, the way people do. There is whispering in corridors as I wheel by, my pedals gleaming. I make out phrases like *so much promise*, and *that's what happens when*. The upshot is, men find me irresistible, they cannot help riding me around the block, stroking my wheels, my derailleur, admiring the sleek line of my down shaft. How the other women envy me now, how I love to see myself reflected on the curved surface of their eyes. How they seek me out at office parties and ask for dating advice. And every Saturday morning a crowd gathers outside my apartment for a glimpse of my shiny titanium frame, my perfectly oiled chain.

A form of directions

Follow any road long enough and you'll reach the end of something. This is especially true at night, when the sky disappears and you happen upon a man with two bandaged hands. Keep the river at your right flank, the crescent moon two inches above your left shoulder. If you happen upon a tree wandering with its eyes closed between rows of parked cars, fire hydrants, you took a wrong turn. You'll never know whom to trust. The thick grass under your feet absorbs the sound your body makes when it stumbles, falls.

The Invisible Girl can be anything she wants when she doesn't want to be invisible

A snow leopard, a tree, an owl. Her favorite is any winged creature. Bats, dragonflies, bees. The Invisible Girl senses her mother's grief at the Invisible Girl's impermanence. She sees it in the unrelenting length of her mother's hair, her skirt's worn hem. But the Invisible Girl cannot help her invisibility. She longs to be tangible, to know where she ends and the rest of the world begins. She envies the concrete bodies of other girls, their silhouettes, the way light must travel around instead of through them.

If I were an Agatha Christie villain

I'd say I found the key to the house under a flowerpot. The
broken window wasn't my handiwork. I didn't see or hear the
commotion in question, didn't kill the old man in his sleep
by pressing a feather pillow over his face until his fingers
stopped twitching. And that's not blood on my dress. I'd tell
the chief inspector half of the truth, while I served him half
a cup of tea, a dish of crumpets. I would withhold the part
about my affair with the dead woman's husband. It didn't last
long and, as they say, some lies are worth telling. Even Poirot
is not unsympathetic to the plight of young lovers. Then, six
minutes and seventeen seconds before curtain, someone would
discover that the key I found under the flowerpot wasn't to
the house, but a mausoleum.

After the world has ended

Spring and its thorns, its wild geese with rough voices calling
from the sky. Your body banks against mine. We have no
skeletons, we are filled with air. We give names to things—*this
is the door, the bed. This is my lover, his throat, his hand
on my hip.* The grass is an ocean. Evenings after supper we
almost drown in it. Always, the body saves us, the body
and its need for air. *This is what moves us, this is the light
uncoiling like a braid.* See how we breathe in without trying.

A sonnet for the men I didn't love

Listen to the tree's cold breath, see how it's grown
accustomed to solitude. Listen, sound of air filling
brown paper bags. *No strings attached,* just the bone
with its muted warning and the light unwilling
to shine. And the body with all its need, breaking
open at a touch. And how I made love to a man
because he couldn't recall his father's face. Aching
is what the heart knows. I used to collect sand
from everywhere I'd been. If only our atoms
didn't devour themselves. *Kiss my closed eyes,
my sun-dappled breasts.* What I mean is, *plums.
Or chrysanthemums.* I'll say it simply: *the sighs
of dying birds fill the cracks in walls.* What I mean is,
I have bread; bring wine, a dozen red roses.

Origin story 4

My mother told me I was carved from the trunk of a
sycamore tree. I remember her blade whittling my knees, the
planes of my neck and torso. She shaped my lungs, I let out a
breath; the first spears of hunger flickered in my wooden belly.

This is how I learned about regret

I was born with a detachable eye. My mother taught me to
care for it, to pluck my eye from its socket so I could clean it.
Most days after school, my brothers and sisters played with
my eye, flicking it back and forth across the kitchen floor
like a marble. Sometimes my mother made them give it back.
Sometimes I searched for days before I found my eye in a bag
of frozen peas, or in the pocket of my sister's sweater stuck
to a half-chewed mint. Afterwards I sat at the kitchen table,
polished my eye with a rag dipped in beeswax, the way my
mother taught me. Back then only my family knew about my
detachable eye but now things are different. Now I date a man
who takes long showers. Sometimes I join him, my eye resting
in a soap dish on the bathroom vanity. I cling to his wet body,
my head on his shoulder, watching my eye watching us, like it
belongs to someone else.

The required assembly

I have eight lovers, one for each day of the week, plus a spare. I keep them in cardboard boxes, holes cut for windows, feed them a diet high in saturated fat. They're never hungry for much. They've learned to speak in each others' voices, like a swarm of pollen-soaked bees. I tell them all they're my favorite, let each one talk uninterrupted when we're in bed. They say things like *if sorrows were crocuses, we could pull them up by the roots* and *if wishes were trees, we'd all be wandering naked in the forest*. I just listen. What do I know, I'm only one ninth of a whole, one crack zig-zagging the white plaster of a wall. *If we lived at the bottom of the ocean, the water's surface would be the sky.*

Notes on grief

Try this: close your eyes and imagine the sea, its unabashed violence. The difference between the wind in my hair and the wind in trees. The difference between what I want, what I'll never have. See how the mouth closes, smooths into a straight line. See the white edges of a wave. And on the table, a bouquet of half-eaten apples and a lullaby. The dead leave us fragments, follow the trail. Try this: close your eyes and imagine the sea where it meets the sky; disappear into the seam.

How to eat an ice floe

The trick is to relax, allow your body to rest as though the freezing water is a feather bed. Don't fight the creep of cold, slow numbing of limbs. Imagine you're a tree in winter, imagine your fingers are leaves. Let them fall. Let the ice floe come to you. As it nears, gnash your teeth, swivel your jaw the way an athlete stretches the muscles of her quadricep, hamstring. Take small bites of ice you can close your mouth around, let the heat from your tongue do the work. Don't swallow until there's enough water in your mouth to drown in. Think of paper lanterns you made as a child, bowls of flickering light set afloat. Think of the moon, how it mirrors the heart in all things. Think of how the heart is a bell, a telephone ringing.

Another one about the birds

Blackbirds mate while flying. Observe how they soar in tacit synchronicity, a large black kite with four wings. Behind the barn there's a patch of grass shaped like a human body. If you think this is some version of the truth, you're half right. That is to say, I knew a man who swallowed a bird. In spite of what you've heard, it was an accident. He only opened his mouth to say something, might have been *shawl*, or *arc*. Once in, there was nothing we could do but wait for the change, the inevitable absorption. He talks now of how he wakes with the memory of flight and the tops of trees, blood pulsing to the frenzied beat of wings.

Bible passages

The vicar, walking into his church for Mass on Sunday morning, was surprised to discover a large, frilly bed where the altar should have been. It was, moreover, an unmade bed, a bed whose occupants were still in it, engaged in activity that the vicar considered lewd. According to news reports, beds with occupants intact have been popping up in churches all over the country. No conclusive answers have been found for the apparating bed epidemic, as it has come to be known, though several theories have been advanced. Many believe the beds are a directive from god to have more sex. The vicar, of course, believes the answer lies in his bible, sitting on his desk next to a half-full decanter of brandy. A narrow beam of light slants across the desk illuminating the leather cover like a pointer. Small particles of dust rise from it, the vicar knows these are the souls of angels ascending towards heaven. Sipping his brandy, the vicar fingers the bible's gilded pages, searches for passages to read to the couples tangled up in bed.

The Invisible Girl goes to confession

When the Invisible Girl goes to confession the priest thinks
she's an angel. He knows she's near when candles on the altar
flicker. If he squints, the priest can see the outline of a woman
rising from the incense. In his dreams the Invisible Girl looks
like Mary Magdalene, with black hair, high cheekbones,
rounded hips. The Invisible Girl's confession is the susurration
of leaves on a windy day. She asks the priest if her invisibility
is a punishment or simply god's way of teaching her humility.
The priest is full of his own questions. In his dreams he is more
man than priest. When he closes his eyes, he pretends that the
Invisible Girl's collarbone is a tree branch and his lips are birds.

The art of leaving

I'd like to be remembered for the way I leave—a room, a taxi,
a man, doesn't matter which. My mother warned me against
this, *you know what they say about girls who are always
leaving.* When I left the last man, I knew I'd write about it one
day. I wore a red hat as I hauled my suitcase out to the car.
Sometimes, the breath just happens, keeps on happening for
a while, like a flashing light in a storm. When I say breath, I
mean sky. When I say storm, I mean telephone. Once, I tried
to become a tree in the wind but my arms tired after only two
days. My mother warned me, *you know what they say about
girls who try to become trees in the wind.*

How to know when I'll be back

Lie awake and stare at the dark, rough-edged like an ink blot.
Be someone's version of Roman Catholic, remember the story of
a man's body pulled from the river. *I am made of brick*, he said
when they hauled him up, six days after he went missing. You'll
think of this later as nothing, a sweep of tongue, a bird the color
of tar, black molasses. I knew a man who carried his heart in a
cardboard box, the why of it is anyone's guess. At parties it was
a great conversation starter. *Hold a penny on your tongue*, he'd
say, *if you want the taste of blood in your mouth.*

The babies

When Mother returns from work one evening, the babies are gone from their cribs. She decides to fix supper while waiting for them to come home. As she walks through the house, tiny flowers spring up from the floorboards between her toes. Mother bends to examine their delicate petals. She sees they are not flowers but the tiny pink mouths of infants. When Mother rests a hand on the wall, little mouths sprout under her fingers. She traces their soft lips with her thumb, thinks of a lullaby.

Soon the whole house is covered with small pink mouths, like buds. In the kitchen, Mother ties an apron around her waist, hums while she cracks eggs, sifts flour into a bowl. The back door opens and Father walks in with his briefcase, wiping his feet on the mat. The door slams behind him and immediately, hundreds of tiny mouths begin to wail and shriek. Mother turns with hands on her hips. "Now you've done it," she says.

Postcard to an old lover

What I want from the sun is its heat, filling me the way water fills a glass. What I want from the salt-colored bones of your body is mercy, the kind you get from a touch. What I want is to reach inside your chest, rap my knuckles against your heart like a door. I'll wait for an answer. I'll be a river rushing past your gaze while you try to keep up. I'll be a bird's shadow, a cross skimming over the ground. The air is full of something we've lost, like your cupped hands filled with darkness. What I want is to climb inside them, pull you in after me.

The encumbrance

The woman with an empty birdcage on her head walks down
my street at 6 every evening. She's never late. *Have you seen
my songbird?* she asks people she meets. Tonight she's sitting
on a park bench, feeding pigeons, telling anyone who'll listen
about the apocalypse. *How many hands do you think god
has?* is a question she likes to ask. It is January, cold enough
to sell the gold in your teeth for a warm coat. The pigeons
have stopped cooing. The woman with a birdcage on her head
has a scarf around her neck, it's the bright yellow of a finch.
We're all pretending to be someone else. The heart of a person
in love is a fish gasping for air. If you stand close enough,
you'll hear the sound of waves like a conch shell at your ear.

Origin story 5

My mother told me I was cut from a bolt of cloth, mirrored halves of my body splayed open on her sewing table. She traced my skull, measured my arms and legs. Finally, she stitched me closed, black seams crisscrossing my palms, the backs of my calves, like tiny railroad tracks.

Genus and Species

The package directions state that *peniculum ariosa*[1] grows best in indirect light. I've planted the seeds under a large acacia tree, next to the begonias. Although they don't require daily watering, the instructions advise talking to them regularly ". . . for encouragement." They must be coaxed to venture out of the ground, out of the perpetual night they have known, like newborns coming into the world. *Peniculum ariosa* flowers up to six times a year. Its flowers are a riot of vivid purples, reds, greens. Their unique hue makes them ideal for use in clothing dyes. Every evening I sit beside them on the grass with a glass of wine, tell them the latest news, my plans for the weekend, the vacation to Seychelles that I'm saving for. They listen, stems quivering, as if in understanding.

---

[1] *Peniculum ariosa* is commonly known as the penis plant, due to the size and shape of the stem, and its propensity to double or triple in length.

The women who grew on trees

There was a time not long ago when women grew on trees.
They started off as tiny pods, thick brown leaves protecting
their translucent skin as they matured. Like plums, they grew
buxom with age, sheltered from the sun and rain. When the
women were ripe they uncurled themselves, dropped from their
vines to stand in the gaps between trees. As the sun fell on their
bodies for the first time they opened the palms of their hands,
turned their faces, their bellies, breasts, to the light.

My great-great grandmother came from an old, venerable line
of tree women. I still remember how she smelled of wet earth,
how on hot summer nights she shed her clothes and slept
outdoors, skin shimmering like pearls under the moon.

What the dead know

The dead hold all the sadness of the living inside their
perpetually closed mouths. They speak without moving their
lips as only the dead can. Not all rivers run to the sea, some
veer off in a kind of desperate searching. The dead know this,
they warn whoever listens, whispers like the creaking of old
trees. You can tell the dead anything. You can tell the dead
how the fullness of the moon fills you with hunger, like the
craving of fire for dry wood, a ship's hull for the open sea.
And all the things you didn't say when you had the chance,
you can say them to the space in an empty room, a name
carved in stone.

The Invisible Girl is a knifepoint against your throat

She's the hush next to a hospital bed, the calm beside a
grave. She's all the names of the dead rolled into one low-
pitched hum. The Invisible Girl knows every story begins
with someone leaving, someone else pleading, *don't go*. She's
the shock on the face of the dying, the film of ice on a park
bench, a flickering lightbulb. Like saints burned at the stake,
the Invisible Girl is a door to the afterlife. Silence grows in her
like a bowl of clear, still water.

The Pawn Shop

People walk in and out at all hours. *How much for a brass lamp, a filigreed screen? How much for a gold tooth?* Above the city, crows fly in haphazard arcs, black slashes of paint against the sky's vast canvas. Once, I lived in this city. Once, I made love to a man with a bird's body. I remember the thick beak protruding from the middle of his face. Afterwards, we stood at the window. I leaned against his feathered chest, his wings caressed my breasts. We watched the city go up in flames, I can still feel the heat rising. *How much for a thick black coat, a wedding ring? How much for a plump juicy soul?*

After a line in a poem by Laura Kasischke

*Like a woman walking down the road with an armful of
roses*, we wore nothing but cool morning wrapped around our
bodies. One of us was always in love with the other. The first
time our hands pressed together in the dark, palm to palm.
I wanted to sleep so I could wake to you. One of us wanted
something more than the night sky, its handful of stars,
the scent of lilacs in the air. Once, you dragged me out in a
summer storm, just to kiss me. *Romantic*, you said *like in the
movies*. Remembering, a kind of surrender. Time is a ball of
string I wind around my fingers. The mist, the other you, the
other I. The dusk, its small yellow flowers, the breeze lifting
strands of hair at my nape.

The craving

What's intimacy, but the scent rising from your skin when the shirt's pulled over your head. This familiar place. This blood trying to speak. I know where the wind goes to die. What we have in common wouldn't fill a single shelf in the pantry. I know how to fashion birds from papier mâché. I line them up on the windowsill, so close to what they'll never have. When I open my mouth you'll hear it, the sudden rush of water like a flood of gray birds spilling from the sky.

I'm beginning to think of the body as a well

To prove my love, I let you bury me in the field beyond the
house. *Close your eyes,* you said, but I couldn't. I still see
your face looming over me as I lay in the ground at your feet,
remember your shirtless back, your hands like points of light.
This body, a dark fevered thing. You used the shovel aunt
Helen gave you, with the blue handle, poured dirt on my body
one slow, small clump at a time. The earth was wet from rain.
You spread it over my belly, neck, lips, weighed down my
eyelids with it. I understood tenderness, then.

Where Snow White is laid to rest

Horses in the field and whippoorwill sing. The dwarves go on as before, each day spent chipping away with pickaxes. They don't know what to do with the empty place at the table, the pile of half-knitted sweaters. Every evening, they gather near the glass coffin in the clearing, all they're left with now are the details. The rise and fall of her chest, the sharp protuberance of hipbones, knees, blue and yellow flowers on her dress. Oak trees mottled with lichen, creaking in the wind. The tips of their cigarettes glow brighter than the fireflies at dusk.

The education

Everything I know about mourning, I learned from my
father. A professional mourner like his father before him, he
knew thirty-three different ways of appearing desolate. Most
people only know four. We lived above the mortuary. The
corpses never bothered me, they were easy to get along with
and didn't mind the dark. We went to funerals every day,
my father was the best mourner. One of the great benefits of
our work—we never had to worry about food. It was always
catered, there was usually baked brie, pâté on toast points,
two different kinds of champagne. My father said his favorite
part of a funeral was the women. They always smiled at him
as they walked by in their black silk dresses, made him think
of sailboats on a summer night gliding on the water.

The most important question

If I tell you about the woman who discovered a beating heart
in a pile of dead leaves, it's really a story about not wanting
to be found. What do you call a mirror that doesn't reflect?
A chair? The trouble with chairs—they don't work well as
flotation devices when the boat is sinking. Actually it wasn't
a beating heart she discovered but a rusty can of nails. It's
a mistake anyone could make. Sometimes you just have to
fill your lungs and pray for buoyancy. If I tell you about the
moon halving itself, growing full again, it's really about a
woman dressing, undressing. I've tried every trick I know,
but the days still follow me wherever I go, like a dog I once
owned.

The sainthood

Take the wings from your back, place them in the reliquary.
Let priests in their white robes anoint your eyelids, the soles
of your feet, your upturned palms. Something sacred must be
burned. The shadows of pilgrims kneel before you in prayer.
Someone presses his lips to your feet. Someone else whispers,
not all gods are edible.

The catechism

Give me a pebble to close my fist around. My hand is harsh
and lonely. If you don't have a pebble, give me an unhatched
egg stolen from a nest. What do you call the sound of water
filling a bathtub? It's kinder to turn the lights off when you
leave a room, especially if someone's still in it. Most people
prefer obscurity. What do you call a voice in the middle of the
night asking if you've lost something? There's a bird trapped
inside my ribcage. If you press your ear to my chest, you'll
hear the flap of its wings.

The Invisible Girl knows

The Invisible Girl knows every shadow is a colony of bees and
every cottonwood tree is haunted. She knows that windmills
on a moor are someone's urgent hands, and the body is
a blade of grass in the wind that sings at night. And the
Invisible Girl knows *a pocketful of ghosts* is a metaphor for
seagulls folding their wings like the shutters of an abandoned
house, the waves patiently gathering every broken husk and
carapace.

Origin story 6

My mother told me I was born from a handful of brushstrokes
on canvas. I remember the swish of her paintbrush as she
outlined my lips, nostrils. She painted my eyes last. In this
version, ghosts gather in every doorway, their murmurs like
the thrum of insects, moonlit and coarse.

Acknowledgments

I am deeply grateful to the following journals and anthologies, where some of these poems first appeared, in the same or slightly different form:

A Cast-Iron Aeroplane That Can Actually Fly, Editor Peter Johnson: "This is how I learned about regret"

The Adirondack Review: "What the dead know"

DMQ Review: "A Sonnet for the Men I Didn't Love"

Fugue: "After the World Has Ended"

Hayden's Ferry Review: Origin stories 1, 2 and 3 previously appeared as "Origin story"

Hotel Amerika: "Desire"

Lake Effect: "Another one about the birds," "Sometimes I want to tell you"

The Laurel Review: "Places of Worship," "Subversion," "The only version we agree on"

Mercurius Magazine: "Invention of dreams"

Michigan Quarterly Review: "Between the Wars," "The Statues"

The Midwest Quarterly Review: "The required assembly"

The Normal School: "Ascension"

ONLYPOEMS: "The education," "Where Snow White is laid to rest," "Origin story 4," "Origin story 5," "The mannequin," "One year I lived alone," "There was a time this could have been true," and "The Invisible Girl goes to confession"

Poets and Artists: "The women who grew on trees," "Genus and Species," "The Crow," "The Pawn Shop," "Exodus"

Short Form Creative Writing, a Writer's Guide and Anthology, Editors H.K. Hummel and Stephanie Lennox: "The Invisible Girl can be anything she wants when she doesn't want to be invisible"

Wherewithal: "The Bicycle"

Notes

Page 22—The title, "Homicide victims rarely talk to police," is a newspaper headline from a February 2009 edition of the *Express Times*. https://freakonomics.com/2012/12/homicide-victims-rarely-talk-to-police-and-other-horrible-headlines/

Page 50—The first line of "After a line in a poem by Laura Kasischke" is taken from her poem "Interruption," appearing in the book *Lilies Without* (Ausable Press, 2007).

The Required Assembly is Shivani Mehta's second book. She is also the author of *Useful Information for the Soon-to-Be Beheaded: Prose Poems*. Her poems have appeared in numerous literary journals. Originally from Singapore, Shivani moved to New York to attend Hamilton College. She later earned her Juris Doctor from Syracuse University. Shivani lives in Los Angeles with her husband and two children, where, along with her husband, she owns and manages a business.

www.ingramcontent.com/pod-product-compliance
Lightning Source LLC
Chambersburg PA
CBHW021511090426
42739CB00007B/568